First World War

and Army of Occupation

War Diary

France, Belgium and Germany

46 DIVISION
139 Infantry Brigade,
Brigade Trench Mortar Battery
2 March 1916 - 28 February 1919

WO95/2695/4

The Naval & Military Press Ltd
www.nmarchive.com
Published in association with The National Archives

Published by

The Naval & Military Press Ltd

Unit 10 Ridgewood Industrial Park,

Uckfield, East Sussex,

TN22 5QE England

Tel: +44 (0) 1825 749494

www.naval-military-press.com

www.nmarchive.com

This diary has been reprinted in facsimile from the original. Any imperfections are inevitably reproduced and the quality may fall short of modern type and cartographic standards.

Contents

War Diary	Ligny-Les-Aire	01/04/1917	13/04/1917
War Diary	Noeux-Les-Mines	14/04/1917	30/04/1917
War Diary	Bully-Grenay	01/05/1917	30/06/1917
War Diary		01/07/1917	03/07/1917
War Diary	Frevillers	04/07/1917	23/07/1917
War Diary	Fouquieres	24/07/1917	31/07/1917
War Diary		01/07/1917	03/07/1917
War Diary	Frevillers	04/07/1917	23/07/1917
War Diary	Fouquieres	21/07/1917	31/07/1917
War Diary		01/08/1917	17/08/1917
War Diary	Fouquieres	20/08/1917	20/08/1917
War Diary	Drouvin	21/08/1917	31/08/1917
War Diary		01/09/1917	18/09/1917
War Diary	La Bourse	19/09/1917	30/09/1917
War Diary		01/10/1917	31/10/1917
War Diary		01/11/1917	30/11/1917
War Diary		01/12/1917	31/12/1917
War Diary		11/12/1917	11/12/1917
War Diary	139th Inf. Bde 46th Div. 139th Trench Mortar Battery. January to December 1918.		
Heading	British Salonika Force War Diary. 28th Division.		
War Diary		01/01/1918	23/01/1918
War Diary	Burbure	24/01/1918	31/01/1918
War Diary		01/02/1918	28/02/1918
War Diary	Laires	01/03/1918	06/03/1918
War Diary	Beuvry	07/03/1918	13/04/1918
War Diary	Vaudricourt	13/04/1918	31/01/1919
War Diary	Prisches	01/02/1919	28/02/1919
War Diary		01/02/1919	28/02/1919
Operation(al) Order(s)	139 Infantry Brigade Warning Order No.232 App I	14/02/1919	14/02/1919
Miscellaneous	March Table To Accompany 139 Brigade Order No. 233.		
Operation(al) Order(s)	139 Brigade Order No. 233. App I	17/02/1919	17/02/1919
Miscellaneous	5th Sherwood Foresters		
Heading	1/5 Nott & Derby Regt Vol 12		
Miscellaneous	139th M. G Coy		
Heading	1/5 Nott & Derby Regt Vol XI		
Miscellaneous	1/8 Notts & Derby Regt Feb Vol XII		
Miscellaneous	8th Sherwood Foresters		
Miscellaneous	1/8 Notts & Derby Regt Vol XIV		
Miscellaneous	1/8 Notts & Derby Vol XIII		
Miscellaneous	139 Bde M Gun Coy Vol II		
Miscellaneous	139 Bde M G Coy Vol III		
Miscellaneous	139 Bde M. Gun Coy Feb Vol I		

W095/2695/(4)

W095/2695 (4)

46TH DIVISION
139TH INFY BDE

TRENCH MORTAR BATTERY

~~JLY~~ MAR 1916-FEB 1919

Instructions regarding War Diaries and Intelligence Summaries are contained in F. S. Regs., Part II. and the Staff Manual respectively. Title Pages will be prepared in manuscript.

WAR DIARY
or
INTELLIGENCE SUMMARY
(Erase heading not required.)

Army Form C. 2118.

139/1 Trench Mortar Battery
139 Inf. Brigade

Place	Date	Hour	Summary of Events and Information	Remarks and references to Appendices
[illegible]	2/3/16		139/1 Trench Mortar Battery formed for 139 Infty Brigade.	
			2 officers Lieut A.B. [illegible] 6th S.F., and 2nd Lt. [illegible] 8th S.F.	
			O.R. 6 from the 5th S.F.	
			5 6th S.F.	
			7 7 S.F.	
			3 8	
Mont St Eloi	9/3/16		Battery moved to Mont St Eloi on 9/3/16 and was attached to 139 Inf Brigade.	
	22/3/16		Battery went into the trenches. The same night a mine was exploded in the sector held by the 5th S.F. The following night support was given by this Battery during the attack of the 5th S.F. to regain the crater.	

[illegible] 2Lt
O.C. 139/1 T.M. Bty.
31/3/16

2449 Wt. W14957/M90 750,000 1/16 J.B.C. & A. Forms/C.2118/12.

Instructions regarding War Diaries and Intelligence Summaries are contained in F. S. Regs., Part II. and the Staff Manual respectively. Title Pages will be prepared in manuscript.

WAR DIARY
or
~~INTELLIGENCE SUMMARY~~
(Erase heading not required.)

Army Form C. 2118.

139/1 T.M. Btty.
139 Bde.

Place	Date	Hour	Summary of Events and Information	Remarks and references to Appendices
Mont. St. Eloi	5/4/16		Mine exploded by enemy in front of the sector held by the 5th Sherwood Foresters. A trench mortar of this battery was at once placed in position so that fire could be brought to bear on enemy in rear of crater, if called upon. On succeeding days it was possible with this gun to damage new work of the enemy in rear of crater.	
	7/4/16		Two collars were cracked on the gun owing to the extreme softness of the ground & the base plate slipping thereby. ~~From position~~ Trench Mortars used to fire on loopholes & were also an effective retaliation to Rifle Grenading.	
	16/4/16		Two mines exploded by us and in each case a Stokes Mortar was detailed to fire on the enemy's front line trench 100 yds right and left respectively of the place where the mines were exploded, while the infantry were seizing the near lip. These Mortars were also to take on any Machine Gun firing on our attacking Infantry. Only one gun ~~proved~~ available & that was able render support in the attack on the crater by the 8th Sherwood Foresters.	
	19/4/16		Mine exploded by the enemy in front of the sector held by the 8th Sherwood Foresters. Stokes Gun placed next day in position to fire on crater.	
	20/4/16		Battery relieved by the 7/1 and 7/2 T.M. Btty, 7th Bde & took over from them billets vacated by them at Bethencourt, the 139/1 Battery going in Corps Reserve. Battery moved to Averdoingt taking over billets vacated by the T.M. Btty of the 138 Bde.	

[illegible] Wallis Lt.
O.C. 139/1 T.M. Bty

2449 Wt. W14957/M90 750,000 1/16 J.B.C. & A. Forms/C.2118/12.

TM XLVI

139/2 T M Bty

Vol 1 + 2

Army Form C. 2118.

Instructions regarding War Diaries and Intelligence Summaries are contained in F. S. Regs., Part II. and the Staff Manual respectively. Title Pages will be prepared in manuscript.

WAR DIARY
or
INTELLIGENCE SUMMARY

(Erase heading not required.)

Place	Date	Hour	Summary of Events and Information	Remarks and references to Appendices
Ligny-St-Flochel 3rd Army School	21/4/16		139/2 Trench Mortar Battery formed by 139th Infantry Brigade. 2 Officers. 2/Lieut- J.R.L. Hunt 5th Sherwood Foresters and 2/Lieut F.B. Gamble 7th Sherwood Foresters. O.R. 5 from 5th S.F. 7 " 6th " 5 " 7th " 5 " 8th "	
Averdoingt	29/4/16		Battery moved to Averdoingt on 29/4/16 with 2 Guns and was attached to 139th Inf. Brigade.	
"	4/5/16		Battery took part in Manouvres with 139th Brigade on ground at Sinèque.	
Canettemont	6/5/16		Battery moved to Canettemont.	
Gaudiempré	7/5/16		" " " Gaudiempré.	
Bienvillers-au-bois.	15/5/16		" " " Bienvillers-au-Bois being placed at the disposal of C.R.A. for digging for 2" T.M.B.	
"	18/5/16		Two other Guns arrived from 3rd Army School.	
Fonquevillers	19/5/16		Battery moved to Fonquevillers taking over from 137/2 T.M.B.	
{from to	25/5/16 31/5/16}		Digging emplacements for 3" Stokes Trench Mortar.	

31/5/16

J.R.L. Hunt 2/Lieut.-
O.C. 139/2 T.M. Battery.

2449 Wt. W14957/M90 750,000 1/16 J.B.C. & A. Forms/C.2118/12.

Instructions regarding War Diaries and Intelligence Summaries are contained in F. S. Regs., Part II. and the Staff Manual respectively. Title Pages will be prepared in manuscript.

WAR DIARY
or
~~INTELLIGENCE SUMMARY~~
(Erase heading not required.)

Army Form C. 2118.

139/1 Trench Mortar Battery
139 Inf. Bde.

Vol

Place	Date	Hour	Summary of Events and Information	Remarks and references to Appendices
Averdoingt	4/5/16		Battery took part in manoeuvres with 139 Bde, during which an attack under cover of smoke was practiced. at Tangues.	
Canettemont	6/5/16		Battery moved to Canettemont.	
Gaudiempré	7/5/16		" " Gaudiempré	
Bienvillers-au-Bois	15/5/16		" " " Bienvillers-au-Bois, being placed at the disposal of the C.R.A. for digging positions for the 2" Trench Mortar Battery 46th Div.	
Fonquevillers	19/5/16		" " Fonquevillers, taking over from the 137/1 Trench Mortar Battery. The guns of the 137/1 T.M.Bty. were left at Fonquevillers & taken over by this Battery, the 139/1 T.M.Bty guns being left at Bienvillers-au-Bois & taken over by the 137/1 T.M.Bty	
	24/5/16		One gun taken into the line & fired test shots	
	From 25/5/16 to 31/5/16		Digging emplacements for Stokes gun.	

A.B.Wallis Lt.
O.C. 139/1 T.M. Bty
31/5/16.

2449 Wt. W14957/M90 750,000 1/16 J.B.C. & A. Forms/C.2118/12.

Attached

139th Trench Mortar Battery

Re. War Diary for June — August 28th 1916

To/ D.A.G.

We have no records from which we can compile a war diary for the month of June. The deceased officers having left no records

Army Form C. 2118.

Vol 5 46

Instructions regarding War Diaries and Intelligence Summaries are contained in F. S. Regs., Part II. and the Staff Manual respectively. Title Pages will be prepared in manuscript.

WAR DIARY
or
~~INTELLIGENCE SUMMARY~~
(Erase heading not required.)

Place	Date	Hour	Summary of Events and Information	Remarks and references to Appendices
Fonquevillers	1/7/16	7.30 am	6 guns ordered to advance in rear of 4th wave of attacking troops with a view to making position in the enemy's lines to bombard pre-arranged points, in the Enemy's 2nd & 3rd lines. Two guns reached the Enemy's wire but unable thro' casualties to come into action. 4 guns were put out of action at the commencement of the advance. Two guns were posted in our front line to bombard the enemy's; also put out of action	
"	2nd	10. pm.	Relieved. Marched back to Warlincourt. Attached 139th M.G. Coy.	
Saulty	3rd		Battery moved to Saulty.	
Bellacourt	11th		Battery moved to Bellacourt.	
"	21st		Battery placed at disposal of C.R.A for digging 2" T.M.B Position	

August. 2nd 1916

E. Jones 2nd Lieut
O.C. 139. Trench Mortar Bty.

2449 Wt. W14957/M90 750,000 1/16 J.B.C. & A. Forms/C.2118/12.

Instructions regarding War Diaries and Intelligence Summaries are contained in F. S. Regs., Part II. and the Staff Manual respectively. Title Pages will be prepared in manuscript.

WAR DIARY
or
~~INTELLIGENCE SUMMARY~~

(Erase heading not required.)

Army Form C. 2118.

Dupl

Place	Date	Hour	Summary of Events and Information	Remarks and references to Appendices
Bellacourt	Aug 1st		2nd Lt. E Jones, 2nd Lt. C H Mickey, 2nd Lt C H Hicks, 2nd Lt W B Davies, 2nd Lt R. O Wallis, + 12 O.R. attached to the Battery after T.M. Course at 3rd Army School. ~~2nd Lt E Jones [illegible]~~ Training + trench fatigues being carried on well	
"	Aug 6		2nd Lt E Jones took over command of the Battery.	
"	Aug 9 to Aug 14		The Battery was placed at the disposal of the Div. T.M. Officer for work.	
"	Aug 15 to " 24th		Preparing gun positions in advanced posts from front line.	
"	" 21st		4 guns 2 Off. 12 O.R. took over positions in trenches.	
"	Aug 24th	11.30pm.	Two guns bombarded enemy's saps and front line between them from 8th Batt's front. 98 rounds fired it was thought some amount of damage was done as repairing was heard the following night. No retaliation. One shell jammed in barrell of gun thro' carriage containing pressing. Legs of an old pattern gun buckled.	
"	Aug 27th		Party already in trenches relieved.	
	Aug 28th " 31.		Preparing new gun emplacements.	

W.B. Davies 2nd Lt.
for O.C. 139th Trench Mortar Battery

2449 Wt. W14957/M90 750,000 1/16 J.B.C. & A. Forms/C.2118/12.

Instructions regarding War Diaries and Intelligence Summaries are contained in F. S. Regs., Part II. and the Staff Manual respectively. Title Pages will be prepared in manuscript.

WAR DIARY
or
INTELLIGENCE SUMMARY
(Erase heading not required.)

Army Form C. 2118.

139 T M Bty

Vol 7

Place	Date	Hour	Summary of Events and Information	Remarks and references to Appendices
Bellacourt	Sept 1		Work on new Gun emplacements	
"	Sept 2	4 P.m	Relief of men in the trenches no firing was done by the Battery	
"	Sept 2nd to Sept 10th		Work on new Gun emplacements	
"	Sept 10th	4. P.m	Relief of men in the trenches, only two shots were fired to register on the enemy's front line, the second shot appeared to fall in the enemy's front line trench	
"	Sept 11 to Sept 15		Work on Gun emplacements	
"	Sept 16		Relief of men in the trenches	
	Sept 16 to Sept 20.		Improving Gun emplacements	
"	Sept 21	2-30 P.m	Registered on the enemy's front line & saps with 4 guns	
"	Sept 22	12:15 am	Battery took part in the short but sharp bombardment just before the raid on the morning of the 22nd inst 5 prisoners were captured.	
Grosville	Sept 24	2-30 P.	Battery moved to Grosville	
	Sept 25 to Sept 28		Work on reserve Gun emplacements	
"	Sept 29	10-30 P.m	30 rounds were fired from the River Bed on the "BLOCKHOUSE" SAP & front line. 1 mortar also fired 44 rounds from "DERBY SAP" on the enemy's front line	
"	Sept 30		Work on Gun Emplacements	

A. J. Cook, 2/Lt
for O. C. 139. Trench Mortar Battery

2449 Wt. W14957/M90 750,000 1/16 J.B.C. & A. Forms/C.2118/12.

Instructions regarding War Diaries and Intelligence Summaries are contained in F. S. Regs., Part II. and the Staff Manual respectively. Title Pages will be prepared in manuscript.

Vol 8 46

Army Form C. 2118.

WAR DIARY
or
~~INTELLIGENCE SUMMARY~~

(Erase heading not required.)

139th T. M. Batty (46 Div)

Place	Date	Hour	Summary of Events and Information	Remarks and references to Appendices
Grosville	Sep 30/Oct 1st		30 Rounds were fired from the RIVER BED on the enemy's BLOCKHOUSE SAP and front line, and 45 Rds were fired from DERBY SAP on the enemy's front line	
"	Oct 2nd to " 8th		Improving Mortar Emplacements, preparing Ammn, and carrying Ammn up to the firing position.	
"	Oct 9th	4.2am	7 Mortars took part in the bombardment of the enemy's trenches and saps on the morning of the 9th inst 700 Rounds were fired.	
"	" 10 to 12 "		Preparing ammunition	
"	13th	10pm	5 Mortars fired on the Enemy's front line & saps, 500 rounds were fired	
"	14 to 18 "		Work on Emplacements, and Physical Training	
"	19 to 23rd		Work on Reserve Emplacements.	
"	24th		Cleaning of dugouts occupied by the Battery in the trenches	
"	25th	9pm	One Mortar and 50 Rds were taken into 'No Man's Land' and the 50 Rounds were fired on the enemy's BLOCKHOUSE SAP.	
"	26th to 28th		Work on Emplacements, and, Cleaning Ammn	
"	29th	10am	Relieved by the 90th T. M. Batty.	
"	30th	10am	Battery left ~~BELLACOURT~~ GROSVILLE, and marched to SUS. St LEGER. arrived there at 4.30pm.	
SUS. St LEGER	31st		Resting, Rifle and Foot inspection.	

E Jones Sec Lieut
Comdg 139th T. M. Batty

2449 Wt. W14957/M90 750,000 1/16 J.B.C. & A. Forms/C.2118/12.

Instructions regarding War Diaries and Intelligence Summaries are contained in F. S. Regs., Part II. and the Staff Manual respectively. Title Pages will be prepared in manuscript.

WAR DIARY
or
~~INTELLIGENCE SUMMARY~~
(Erase heading not required.)

Army Form C. 2118.

Dupl Vol

139th Trench Mortar Battery

Place	Date	Hour	Summary of Events and Information	Remarks and references to Appendices
Sus-St. Leger	1st Nov		Marched from Sus-St Leger to Canteleux.	
Canteleux	2nd "	9 am	Foot and Rifle Inspection	
"	3rd "	8.30am	Marched from Canteleux to Hiermont	
Hiermont	4th "		Training as instructed by Bde H.Qs	
"	5th "		" " " " "	
"	6th "		Marched from Hiermont to Neuville	
Neuville	7th "		Training as instructed by Bde H.Q.	
"	8th "		" " " " "	
"	9th "	7.30pm	Marched from Neuville to St Riquier and embussed for Abbeville	
Abbeville	10th "	3 am	Entrained at Abbeville for Ligny St Flochel, arriving there at 6pm same day.	
Ligny St Flochel	11th " to the 18th	to 12 noon	Training at 3rd Army School of Mortars	
"	18th	2pm	Embussed at Ligny St Flochel for Hiermont, arriving there at 6-30pm.	
Hiermont	19th to 21st		Training under O.C. Battery	
"	22nd		Marched from Hiermont to St Acheul	
St Acheul	23rd	8.30am	" " St Acheul to ~~Occhos~~ Occoches, arriving there at 12-30pm.	
Occoches	24th		Foot and Rifle Inspection	
"	25th	8.30am	Marched from Occoches to Warluzel, arriving there at 1-15 pm	
Warluzel	26th to 30th		Training as per B.R. Orders.	

E. Jones Lieut
Comdg 139th T.M. Batty

2449 Wt. W14957/M90 750,000 1/16 J.B.C. & A. Forms/C.2118/12.

Instructions regarding War Diaries and Intelligence Summaries are contained in F. S. Regs., Part II. and the Staff Manual respectively. Title Pages will be prepared in manuscript.

WAR DIARY
or
~~INTELLIGENCE SUMMARY~~
(Erase heading not required.)

Army Form C. 2118.

Vol 10

139th Trench Mortar Battery

Place	Date	Hour	Summary of Events and Information	Remarks and references to Appendices
Warluzel	1st Dec		Testing and Fitting the Battery with Small Box Respirators	
	2nd "		Bde Ceremonial Drill at Sus St Leger.	
	3rd "		G. O. C. inspection at Sus St Leger.	
"	4th "	9-45am	Marched from Warluzel to Souastre	
Souastre	5th		Half the Battery relieved the half Battery of the 147th Bde in the trenches at Fonquevillers.	
	6th to 31st		2 thirds of the Battery in the trenches at Fonquevillers during this period. 20 to 30 rounds of ammn being fired almost every day in retaliation to enemy Light T. M. and Rifle Grenades.	

A. J. Cook 2/Lt
Offr Comdg 139th T M Batty

2449 Wt. W14957/M90 750,000 1/16 J.B.C. & A. Forms/C.2118/12.

139th Inf Bde
46th Div.

139th Trench Mortar Battery

June to December 191[illegible]

On His Britannic Majesty's Service.

By F.O. Bag.

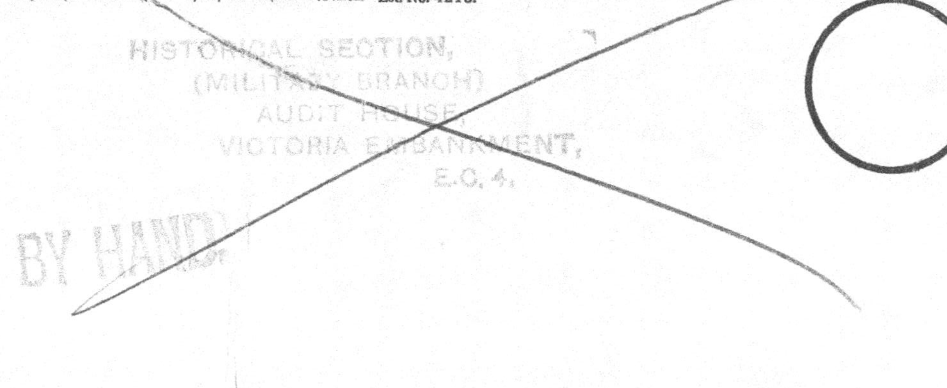
ON HIS MAJESTY'S SERVICE.

NATIONAL ECONOMY. **FASTEN** Envelope by gumming this Label across Flap. **OPEN** by cutting Label instead of tearing Envelope.

(2986.) Wt. 34280/204. 4,000,000. 12/18. P.P.Ltd. Est. No. 4213.

HISTORICAL SECTION,
(MILITARY BRANCH)
AUDIT HOUSE,
VICTORIA EMBANKMENT,
E.C. 4.

BY HAND

Army Form C. 2118.

WAR DIARY
or
INTELLIGENCE SUMMARY

(Erase heading not required.)

139th Trench Mortar Battery

Vol XI

Instructions regarding War Diaries and Intelligence Summaries are contained in F. S. Regs., Part II. and the Staff Manual respectively. Title Pages will be prepared in manuscript.

Place	Date	Hour	Summary of Events and Information	Remarks and references to Appendices
Souastre	1/1/17 to 31/1/17		2 thirds of Battery in the trenches at Fonquevillers during the month, practically all the firing done during this month was in retaliation to enemy trench Mortars and Rifle Grenades. The part of the Battery not in the line, rests at Souastre.	

J Hamilton 2/Lt.

for Officer Comdg 139th T.M. Battery.

2449 Wt. W14957/M90 750,000 1/16 J.B.C. & A. Forms/C.2118/12.

Instructions regarding War Diaries and Intelligence Summaries are contained in F. S. Regs., Part II. and the Staff Manual respectively. Title Pages will be prepared in manuscript.

WAR DIARY
or
INTELLIGENCE SUMMARY

(Erase heading not required.) 139th Trench Mortar Battery

Army Form C. 2118.

Place	Date	Hour	Summary of Events and Information	Remarks and references to Appendices
Foncquevillers	1/2/17 to 19/2/17		In the trenches at Foncquevillers	
"	20/2/17		Relieved by the 138th Trench Mortar Battery, then moved into Souastre	
Souastre	21/2/17	9 am	Left Souastre and marched to Sus St Leger arriving there at 1-5 pm.	
Sus St Leger	22/2/17 to 25/2/17		Training under Bde instruction.	
	26/2/17	9.45 am	Left Sus St Leger and marched to Simencourt arriving there at 3.25 pm.	
Simencourt	27/2/17	4.45 pm	Left Simencourt and marched to Achicourt arriving there at 9.15 pm.	
Achicourt	28/2/17	6.45 pm	Left Achicourt and marched to Fosseux arriving there at midnight.	

N. J. Cork Capt.
Comdg 139th T M Battery.

2449 Wt. W14957/M90 750,000 1/16 J.B.C. & A. Forms/C.2118/12.

Instructions regarding War Diaries and Intelligence Summaries are contained in F. S. Regs., Part II. and the Staff Manual respectively. Title Pages will be prepared in manuscript.

WAR DIARY
or
INTELLIGENCE SUMMARY

(Erase heading not required.) 139th Trench Mortar Battery

Vol 12

Army Form C. 2118.

Place	Date	Hour	Summary of Events and Information	Remarks and references to Appendices
Fonquevillers	1/2/1917 to 19/2/17		In the trenches at Fonquevillers	
"	20/2/17		Relieved by the 138th Trench Mortar Battery, then moved into Souastre	
Souastre	21/2/17	9am	Left Souastre, and marched to Sus, St Leger, arriving there at 1-57 pm.	
Sus St Leger	22/2/17 to 25/2/17		Training under Bde instruction	
"	26/2/17	9.45am	Left Sus St Leger, and marched to Simencourt arriving there at 3.25 pm.	
Simencourt	27/2/17	4.45pm	Left Simencourt, and marched to Achicourt, arriving there at 9.15 pm.	
Achicourt	28/2/17	6.45pm	Left Achicourt and marched to Fosseux, arriving there at midnight.	

N J Cook Lt
Comdg 139th T M Battery.

2449 Wt. W14957/M90 750,000 1/16 J.B.C. & A. Forms/C.2118/12.

Instructions regarding War Diaries and Intelligence Summaries are contained in F. S. Regs., Part II. and the Staff Manual respectively. Title Pages will be prepared in manuscript.

WAR DIARY
or
INTELLIGENCE SUMMARY
(Erase heading not required.)

Army Form C. 2118.

Vol 13

139th Trench Mortar Battery

Place	Date	Hour	Summary of Events and Information	Remarks and references to Appendices
	1/3/17		Marched from Fosseux to Halloy, through Barly, Saulty, Pommera, and Grenas.	
	2/3/17		Marched from Halloy to Saulty, through Famechon, Pas, and Henu	
	3/3/17		Relieved 138th T M Bty at Gommecourt.	
	4/3/17 to 18/3/17		In the line at Gommecourt. And were relieved by the 138th T M Bty on the morning of the 18th, and moved back to Souastre.	
	19/3/17		Resting at Souastre.	
	20/3/17		Marched to Bayencourt.	
	21st & 22nd		At Bayencourt.	
	23/3/17		Marched from Bayencourt to Contay, through Courcelles, Mailly and Vadencourt.	
	24/3/17		Marched from Contay to Villers Bocage, through Beaucourt.	
	25/3/17		Marched from Villers Bocage to Saleux, through Poulainville, Amiens and Salouel.	
	26/3/17		Marched from Saleux to Bacouel, through Vers.	
	27/3/17		Entrained at Bacouel.	
	28/3/17		Detrained at Chocques, and marched to Ligny through Lillers Burecq and St Hilaire.	
	29/3/17 to 31/3/17		At Ligny	

N J Cook Lt
O.C 139th T M Bty

2449 Wt. W14957/M90 750,000 1/16 J.B.C. & A. Forms/C.2118/12.

Army Form C. 2118.

Vol 14

Instructions regarding War Diaries and Intelligence Summaries are contained in F. S. Regs., Part II. and the Staff Manual respectively. Title Pages will be prepared in manuscript.

WAR DIARY
or
INTELLIGENCE SUMMARY
(Erase heading not required.)

Month of April 1917 — 139th Trench Mortar Battery

Place	Date	Hour	Summary of Events and Information	Remarks and references to Appendices
Ligny-les-Aire	1st to 12th		Chiefly Physical Training and lectures on the "Always Fuze". A few rounds were fired on the 10th for ranging practice.	2nd Lt. J. HAMILTON of this Battery was wounded in R foot + leg by shell, on 21/4/17. CORPORAL COPE wounded on 27/4/17 (R foot)
	12th	6.30am	Left Ligny-les-Aire and marched to CHOCQUES, arrived there at 10.50am	
	13th	10.10am	Marched from CHOCQUES to NOEUX-LES-MINES.	
NOEUX-LES-MINES	14th to 17th		Training, Gun Drill, Physical Training etc. (14th Lt. A. J. COOK admitted to hospital)	
	18th		Battery left NOEUX-LES-MINES for ANGRES, Guns were taken on handcarts having got as far as COLONEL'S Hd. they received orders to go back to NOEUX-LES-MINES. On the way back hand-carts and Guns were left at SAINS-EN-GOHELLE, in charge of 1 NCO and 6 men.	
	19th	11am	Again left NOEUX-LES-MINES for ANGRES, collecting Guns and handcarts on the way up. Getting as far as AIX NOULETTE, handcarts had to be left ~~behind~~ there, as the road was very bad between AIX NOULETTE and ANGRES. The guns being carried by the men up to ANGRES. And during the evening relieved the 73rd T.M. Battery	
	20th to 29th		In the trenches near LIEVIN. Rounds fired during period in trenches – 324.	
	30th		Battery relieved by the 137 T.M. Battery, and moved back to BULLY-GRENAY.	

J. Gargate Lt
OC 139 T.M.B.

2449 Wt. W14957/M90 750,000 1/16 J.B.C. & A. Forms/C.2118/12.

Instructions regarding War Diaries and Intelligence Summaries are contained in F. S. Regs., Part II. and the Staff Manual respectively. Title Pages will be prepared in manuscript.

Army Form C. 2118.

WAR DIARY or INTELLIGENCE SUMMARY

(Erase heading not required.)

139th Trench Mortar Battery

Place	Date	Hour	Summary of Events and Information	Remarks and references to Appendices
BULLY-GRENAY	1/5/17 to 5/5/17		Training, Gun Drill, Physical Exercises etc.	6/5/17 2/Lt. S.J.D. BERGER attached from 7th S.F.
	6/5/17	7 pm	Left BULLY to relieve the 138th T.M.B. in the line near LOOS. Relief carried out during the night.	
	7/5/17 to 20/5/17		In the trenches. 15th 16th & 17th preparing for raid by 7th S.F., which took place night 18th/19th. Small parties of enemy attempted to enter our trenches 2 minutes before zero but were driven off by Bombs, at junction of NOVEL TR. & old front line. (N.1a.)	
BULLY-GRENAY	21/5/17 to 25/5/17		At BULLY, training. Relieved the 137th T.M.B. on the night of the 25th.	
	25/5/17 to 31/5/17		In the trenches. 2 O.R's casualties (wounded) during this period, by shell splinters. One gun emplacement blown in.	
			Approx. No. of Rounds fired during month. 1350 rds	

[signature] O.C. 139th T.M. Battery

2449 Wt. W14957/M90 750,000 1/16 J.B.C. & A. Forms/C.2118/12.

Army Form C. 2118.

Instructions regarding War Diaries and Intelligence Summaries are contained in F. S. Regs., Part II. and the Staff Manual respectively. Title Pages will be prepared in manuscript.

WAR DIARY
or
INTELLIGENCE SUMMARY
(Erase heading not required.)

139th Trench Mortar Battery

Place	Date	Hour	Summary of Events and Information	Remarks and references to Appendices
BULLY GRENAY	1/6/17 to 10/6/17		In the trenches - Lieven Sector - 1 Officer Wounded - Lt J. G. Gargale 2 Other ranks killed & 2 Other ranks wounded	12/6/17 Lt. J L PERCIVAL attached from 6th S F
	10/6/17 to 15/6/17		At Bully Grenay - training - Physical Exercises & Gun Drill etc	20/6/17 2 Lt. R H. WOOD attached from 7 S F
	15/6/17 to 30/6/17		Relieved 137 Trench Mortar Battery in - St Pierre Sector 3 Other Ranks wounded 1400 rounds were fired on the night of 24th & 25th when the 6th Sherwood Foresters made a raid under a Trench Mortar Barrage on this Sector of the enemy trenches	30/6/17 2 Lt. W L HILL attached from 5th S F

Approx No of rounds fired during month 5.500 rds

Jno L Percival Lt.
Oc 139 T M Battery

2449 Wt. W14957/M90 750,000 1/16 J.B.C. & A. Forms/C.2118/12.

Army Form C. 2118.

Instructions regarding War Diaries and Intelligence Summaries are contained in F. S. Regs., Part II. and the Staff Manual respectively. Title Pages will be prepared in manuscript.

WAR DIARY
or
INTELLIGENCE SUMMARY

(Erase heading not required.)

139th Trench Mortar Battery

Place	Date	Hour	Summary of Events and Information	Remarks and references to Appendices
	1st to 3rd July 1917		Battery were in the trenches near LOOS. Relieved by the 9th Canadian T M Bty on the night of the 3rd inst, after being relieved Battery were conveyed to FREVILLERS in motor lorries. 4 Handcarts were brought to FREVILLIERS by 139th M G coy transport, the remainder of the handcarts and the guns were carried on motor lorries.	morning of the 4th Btty moved to FREVILLERS
FREVILLERS	4th to 22nd July		At FRÉVILLIERS, Training, Gun Drill, Physical Training, etc. Sports were held by the 6th SHERWOOD FORESTERS, 139th M.G coy, + 139th T M Bty at FREVILLERS, a few prizes were won by the Bty.	
	23rd		Battery moved to FOUQUIÉRES.	
FOUQUIÉRES	24th		Cleaning Guns etc, Physical Drill, + Rifle Exercises.	
	25th		Moved to PHILOSOPHE, and relieved the 71st T.M. Battery.	
	26th to 31st		In the trenches.	
			Approximate number of rounds fired - 2700	

Jno L Percival Lt
Officer Comdg 139th Trench Mortar Battery

2449 Wt. W14957/M90 750,000 1/16 J.B.C. & A. Forms/C.2118/12.

Instructions regarding War Diaries and Intelligence Summaries are contained in F. S. Regs., Part II. and the Staff Manual respectively. Title Pages will be prepared in manuscript.

4

WAR DIARY
or
~~INTELLIGENCE~~ SUMMARY
(Erase heading not required.)

Army Form C. 2118. 46

Vol

139th Trench Mortar Battery

Place	Date	Hour	Summary of Events and Information	Remarks and references to Appendices
	1st to 3rd July 1917		Battery were in the trenches near LOOS. Relieved by the 9th Canadian T.M. Bty on the night of the 3rd inst, after being relieved Battery were conveyed to FREVILLIERS in motor lorries. 4 Handcarts were brought to FREVILLIERS by 139th M G coy transport, the remainder of the handcarts and the guns were carried on motor lorries.	morning of the 4th Battery moved to FREVILLE
FREVILLERS	4th to 22nd July		At FRÉVILLIERS, Training, Gun Drill, Physical Training, etc. Sports were held by the 6th SHERWOOD FORESTERS, 139th M.G. Coy, + 139th T.M. Bty at FREVILLERS, a few prizes were won by the Bty.	
	23rd		Battery moved to FOUQUIÉRES.	
FOUQUIÉRES	24th		Cleaning Guns etc, Physical Drill, + Rifle Exercises.	
	25th		Moved to PHILOSOPHE, and relieved the 7th T.M. Battery.	
	26th to 31st		In the trenches. Approximate number of rounds fired - 2700	

Jno L Percival Lt
Officer Comdg 139th Trench Mortar Battery

2449 Wt. W14957/M90 750,000 1/16 J.B.C. & A. Forms/C.2118/12.

Army Form C. 2118.

Instructions regarding War Diaries and Intelligence Summaries are contained in F. S. Regs., Part II. and the Staff Manual respectively. Title Pages will be prepared in manuscript.

WAR DIARY
or
~~INTELLIGENCE SUMMARY~~
(Erase heading not required.)

139th Trench Mortar Battery

Place	Date	Hour	Summary of Events and Information	Remarks and references to Appendices
	1917 1st August to 16th August		In the trenches East of VERMELLES. Two casualties during this period in the trenches, both slightly wounded. 240310 L/c Wyche A, 202172 Pte Stone W	
	16 August		Battery were relieved by the 138th T.M.B. on the evening of the 16th. After being relieved Battery moved back to rest billets at FOUQUIÉRES.	
FOUQUIÉRES	17th August to 20th August		At FOUQUIERES, training.	
	20th August		Battery moved to DROUVIN.	
DROUVIN	21st August to 25th August		At DROUVIN, training. All Small Box Respirators were tested in Gas Chamber at VAUDRICOURT on the 24th August.	
	25th August	9.30am	Marched to ANNEQUIN, and during the evening relieved the 99th T M Bty, in the line East of CAMBRIN.	
	25th to 31st August		In the trenches East of CAMBRIN.	

John Percival Capt
Officer Commanding 139th T M Battery

2449 Wt. W14957/M90 750,000 1/16 J.B.C. & A. Forms/C.2118/12.

7

Instructions regarding War Diaries and Intelligence Summaries are contained in F. S. Regs., Part II. and the Staff Manual respectively. Title Pages will be prepared in manuscript.

WAR DIARY
or
~~INTELLIGENCE SUMMARY~~
(Erase heading not required.)

Army Form C. 2118. 46

39th Trench Mortar Battery

Vol

Place	Date	Hour	Summary of Events and Information	Remarks and references to Appendices
	1/9/17 to 18/9/17		Battery in the line east of VERMELLES, 7 guns in the line. Daily ammunition expenditure 500 Rds. Numerous emplacements constructed. On the 12th one gun at QUARRY ALLEY was destroyed through enemy shell, detonating ammunition (300 Rds ammonal) large crater caused. On 13th hostile working party dispersed with loss.	During the stay in the line from 1st to 18th the following became casualties: 241060 L/c SMEDLEY.r (6th S.R.) 305104 Pte BETTERIDGE (8th S.R.) 269249 Pte RICHARDSON H. (7th S.R.)
La BOURSE	19/9/17 to 22/9/17		At rest at LA BOURSE. On the night of the 22nd one section of the Battery relieved part of the 71st and 18th T.M.B. in the line east of PHILOSOPHE. the section of the Battery remaining at LA BOURSE.	
	23/9/17		The section at LA BOURSE moved up to MAZINGARBE. in reserve.	
	24/9/17 to 30/9/17		In the HILL 70 Sector. Owing to ammunition difficulties very little firing. Emplacements were started on and Battery HdQrs in RAILWAY ALLEY were constructed.	

Jno. L. Percival Capt.

Officer Commanding 39th T.M. Battery.

2449 Wt. W14957/M90 750,000 1/16 J.B.C. & A. Forms/C.2118/12.

Army Form C. 2118.

Instructions regarding War Diaries and Intelligence Summaries are contained in F. S. Regs., Part II. and the Staff Manual respectively. Title Pages will be prepared in manuscript.

WAR DIARY
or
INTELLIGENCE SUMMARY

(Erase heading not required.)

139th Trench Mortar Battery

Place	Date	Hour	Summary of Events and Information	Remarks and references to Appendices
	1-10-17 to 31-10-17		In the trenches East of PHILOSOPHE	Casualties during the month – 241557 Pte Lindsay slightly wounded
			One Mortar was destroyed by enemy shell fire on the 6th inst.	31/10/17 2/Lt Pearce accidentally wounded
			5 Guns in action –	
	31-10-17		4 Guns barraged Trench on right of daylight raid by 139 Bde –	
			Fired from Zero to Zero+7 – Amm. expended 410 rounds –	
			Ammunition expended during the month 4500 rounds –	

Jno. L. Percival
Capt.
OC 139 TMB

2449 Wt. W14957/M90 750,000 1/16 J.B.C. & A. Forms/C.2118/12.

Instructions regarding War Diaries and Intelligence Summaries are contained in F. S. Regs., Part II. and the Staff Manual respectively. Title Pages will be prepared in manuscript.

WAR DIARY
or
~~INTELLIGENCE SUMMARY~~
(Erase heading not required.)

Army Form C. 2118.

139th Trench Mortar Battery

Place	Date	Hour	Summary of Events and Information	Remarks and references to Appendices
	1-11-17 to 16-11-17		One section of the Battery in the line, HILL 70 Sector, and one section at rest at MAZINGARBE. Those in the trenches were relieved by a section of the 138th T.M.B. on the 16th inst. and afterwards they moved back into new rest billets at LA BOURSE. The section which had been resting at MAZINGARBE, took over in the line EAST of VERMELLES from part of the 138th T.M.B. during the morning of the 16th inst.	*During this period in the line, the following became casualties:- 305413 Pte Foot H (Killed) 25/11/17; 240439 Pte Wheatley W (Wounded) 28/11/17; 201397 Pte Lakbury D. (Wounded) 25/11/17
*	17-11-17 to 30-11-17		One section of the Battery in the line EAST of VERMELLES, and one section at rest at LA BOURSE. Two mortars have been destroyed by shell fire, one on the 18th inst. and the other on the 28th inst.	

Jnoh Percival Capt.

Officer Comdg 139th T. M. Battery

2449 Wt. W14957/M90 750,000 1/16 J.B.C. & A. Forms/C.2118/12.

Instructions regarding War Diaries and Intelligence Summaries are contained in F. S. Regs., Part II. and the Staff Manual respectively. Title Pages will be prepared in manuscript.

WAR DIARY
or
~~INTELLIGENCE SUMMARY~~
(Erase heading not required.)

Army Form C. 2118.

139th Trench Mortar Battery

Place	Date	Hour	Summary of Events and Information	Remarks and references to Appendices
	1-12-17 to 31-12-17		Battery in the line EAST of VERMELLES. One mortar was destroyed by shell fire on the 22nd	Casualties during the month. 240590 Pte T. Garley 6th S.F. (Killed) 22/12/17
	11:12:17		Fired with 8 mortars in support of a Battalion daylight raid carried out by the 5th Sherwood Foresters. Enemy trench junctions, C.Ts and 2nd line on the northern flank of the raid area were fired on; other targets on the northern dummy raid front were engaged. Number of rounds fired - 1500 Cpl. Beale & Pte Bunn awarded the Military Medal in connection with this raid.	240152 Pte W. Harrison 6th S.F. (Wounded) 22/12/17
			On 25/12/17 and 29/12/17 a destructive shoot on enemy T.Ms in co-operation with 4.5" Hows. 6" and 9.45" T.Ms was carried out.	
			During the month gun positions in the line were improved & all fitted with over head cover.	
			Total number of rounds fired during the month 15,311. Daily average. 500	

Jno. h. Percival Capt.
O.C. 139th Trench Mortar Battery

2449 Wt. W14957/M90 750,000 1/16 J.B.C. & A. Forms/C.2118/12.

139th Inf. Bde
46th Div.

139th Trench Mortar Battery.

January to December 1918.

Volume No. ____

BRITISH SALONIKA FORCE

WAR DIARY.

28TH Division

Vol. No.	Unit	PERIOD From	PERIOD To
19.	83RD Machine Gun Company.	1. 11. 17	30. 11. 17
19.	84TH do.	"	"
19.	85TH do.	"	"
3.	277TH do.	"	"

A.P. & S.D., Alex./No. 752/8:5:17/3000 (50041G/53) W. M. & Co.

Instructions regarding War Diaries and Intelligence Summaries are contained in F. S. Regs., Part II. and the Staff Manual respectively. Title Pages will be prepared in manuscript.

4

WAR DIARY
or
~~INTELLIGENCE SUMMARY~~

(Erase heading not required.)

Army Form C. 2118. 46

139th Trench Mortar Battery

Vol

Place	Date	Hour	Summary of Events and Information	Remarks and references to Appendices
	1/1/18 to 22/1/18		Battery in the line EAST OF VERMELLES. The Battery was relieved on the 22nd inst, by the 34th T. M. Bty, after being relieved the Battery moved back into billets at LA. BOURSE.	
	23/1/18		moved from LA BOURSE at 9.30 am, and marched to BURBURE.	
BURBURE	24/1/18 to 31/1/18		Training at BURBURE	

139TH TRENCH MORTAR BATTERY.
No. ....
Date ....

Jno H Percival
Capt
O.C. 139 T.M.B.

2449 Wt. W14957/M90 750,000 1/16 J.B.C. & A. Forms/C.2118/12.

4

Instructions regarding War Diaries and Intelligence Summaries are contained in F. S. Regs., Part II. and the Staff Manual respectively. Title Pages will be prepared in manuscript.

WAR DIARY

~~or~~

~~INTELLIGENCE SUMMARY~~

(Erase heading not required.)

Army Form C. 2118.

46

139th Trench Mortar Battery

Vol

Place	Date	Hour	Summary of Events and Information	Remarks and references to Appendices
	1-2-18 to 7-2-18		Battery was in Training at Burbure. Physical. Gun Drill. Squad Drill. etc.	
	8-2-18		Battery marched to 1st Corps. T.M. School at FOUQUIERES for Instruction passing through Lozinghem Marles-les-Mines. LAPUGNOY. Gosnay.	
	13-2-18		Battery left School and marched to Vedinchel, passing through Chocques. and Lillers.	
	14-2-18		The Battery moved to LAIRES. passing through Livosart. Pafart. and continued with training programme.	
	15/2/18 to 28-2-18		The Battery continued with Training Programme at LAIRES	

for [signature] Berger

O.C. 139 T.M.B.

2449 Wt. W14957/M90 750,000 1/16 J.B.C. & A. Forms/C.2118/12.

Army Form C. 2118.

Instructions regarding War Diaries and Intelligence Summaries are contained in F. S. Regs., Part II. and the Staff Manual respectively. Title Pages will be prepared in manuscript.

WAR DIARY
or
~~INTELLIGENCE SUMMARY~~
(Erase heading not required.)

139th Trench Mortar Battery

Place	Date	Hour	Summary of Events and Information	Remarks and references to Appendices
LAIRES	1/3/18 to 6/3/18		Training. On the afternoon of the 6th inst the Battery embussed at LAIRES for BEUVRY, arrived at BEUVRY about 3.30 pm.	Whilst in the CAMBRIN Sector the following became casualties. 241537 Pte Lindsey H. 22/3/18 and 305116 Pte Parker F. 22/3/18.
BEUVRY	7/3/18 to 13/3/18		Billeted at BEUVRY. Gun Drill, Physical Drill, and Recreational Training were carried out each day.	
	14/3/18		One Section of the Battery moved into the line EAST of CAMBRIN. The other section remained in rest Billets at BEUVRY.	
	15/3/18 to 27/3/18		One Section of the Battery in the line EAST of CAMBRIN. Relieved in this sector by part of the 166th T.M.B. and part of the 32nd T.M.B., on the 27th inst. During the last few days in this Sector the whole Battery was occupied in the construction of reserve gun-positions behind the RESERVE & VILLAGE lines. Eight in all were completed & stocked with ammunition.	
	27/3/18 to 31/3/18		Two thirds of the Battery moved into the line EAST of CITE ST PIERRE (St. EMILE SECTOR). The remainder of the Battery moved into rest Billets at BULLY, on the morning of the 28th inst.	

G D Barger
Lieut.
O.C. 139th T.M. Bty.

2449 Wt. W14957/M90 750,000 1/16 J.B.C. & A. Forms/C.2118/12.

Army Form C. 2118.

Instructions regarding War Diaries and Intelligence Summaries are contained in F. S. Regs., Part II. and the Staff Manual respectively. Title Pages will be prepared in manuscript.

WAR DIARY
or
~~INTELLIGENCE SUMMARY~~

(Erase heading not required.)

139th Trench Mortar Battery

Place	Date	Hour	Summary of Events and Information	Remarks and references to Appendices
	1/4/18 to 11/4/18		In the line EAST of CITE ST PIERRE. On the night of the 11th the Battery was relieved from this sector by the 4th T.M.B. (Canadians) and moved back to BULLY-GRENAY.	
	12/4/18		moved from BULLY-GRENAY to VAUDRICOURT in Buses.	
VAUDRICOURT	13/4/18 to 22/4/18		At VAUDRICOURT	
	23/4/18		Battery relieved the 8th T.M.B in the line EAST of BÈTHUNE	
	24/4/18 to 28/4/18		In the line EAST of BÈTHUNE. Relieved by the 138th T.M.B on the night of the 28th inst, and moved back into rest billets at FOUQUIÈRES	
	29/4/18 to 30/4/18		At FOUQUIÈRES	

Jack Pearce[?]
Captain
Officer Comdg 139th T.M. Bty

2449 Wt. W14957/M90 750,000 1/16 J.B.C. & A. Forms/C.2118/12.

Instructions regarding War Diaries and Intelligence Summaries are contained in F. S. Regs., Part II. and the Staff Manual respectively. Title Pages will be prepared in manuscript.

WAR DIARY
or
~~INTELLIGENCE SUMMARY~~
(Erase heading not required.)

Army Form C. 2118.

139th Trench Mortar Battery

Place	Date	Hour	Summary of Events and Information	Remarks and references to Appendices
	1/5/18 to 3/5/18		AT FOUQUIÉRES.	The following became Casualties on the 9th & 10th – Capt J.L. PERCIVAL M.C. 240538 Sgt Wilshaw D.C.M. 241415 L/C Rudley P. 240310 L/C Wyche A. 265847 Pte Woods F. 378036 Pte Spencer G. 200584 Pte Sanders G. 240439 Pte Wheatley W. 242651 Pte Hall R. 267110 Pte Frampton F. 269[illegible] Pte Harris [illegible] all wounded
	4/5/18 to 11/5/18		Battery in the line EAST of BÉTHUNE, on the night of the 11th inst the Battery were relieved by the 138th T.M. Bty. and moved back to rest billets at FOUQUIÉRES.	
	12/5/18 to 15/5/18		AT FOUQUIÉRES. On the night of the 15th inst the battery moved into the line, and relieved the 137th T.M. Bty.	
	16/5/18 to 26/5/18		Battery in the line EAST of BÉTHUNE. Relieved from this sector by the 137th T.M. Bty on the 26th inst.	
	27/5/18 to 30/5/18		AT FOUQUIÉRES. Relieved the 138th T.M. Bty in the line EAST of BÉTHUNE on the 30th inst.	
	31/5/18		In the line.	

Jno L. Percival
Captain

O.C. 139 T.M.B.

2449 Wt. W14957/M90 750,000 1/16 J.B.C. & A. Forms/C.2118/12.

Army Form C. 2118.

Instructions regarding War Diaries and Intelligence Summaries are contained in F. S. Regs., Part II. and the Staff Manual respectively. Title Pages will be prepared in manuscript.

WAR DIARY
or
~~INTELLIGENCE SUMMARY~~
(Erase heading not required.)

39th Trench Mortar Battery

Place	Date	Hour	Summary of Events and Information	Remarks and references to Appendices
	1:6:18 6:6:18	16	In the line EAST of BETHUNE, relieved from this sector by the 137th T. M. Bty, on the night of the 6th inst:	30685 Pte Clarke W became a casualty wounded and died of wounds on the 20th.
	7:6:18 10:6:18	16	In rest Billets at FOUQUIÈRES, on the night of the 10th Bty moved into the line, and relieved the 138th T. M. B.	
	11:6:18 (18) 18:6:18	16	In the line EAST of BÈTHUNE, relieved by the 137th T. M. Bty on the 18th inst.	
	19:6:18 22:6:18	16	At FOUQUIÈRES. Training, Physical Drill, and Gun Drill. Relieved the 137th T. M. Bty on the 22nd inst.	
	23:6:18 30:6:18	16	In the line EAST of BETHUNE.	

Jno L Percival
Captain.
O. C. 139th T. M. Bty.

2449 Wt. W14957/M90 750,000 1/16 J.B.C. & A. Forms/C.2118/12.

Instructions regarding War Diaries and Intelligence Summaries are contained in F. S. Regs., Part II. and the Staff Manual respectively. Title Pages will be prepared in manuscript.

Army Form C. 2118.

WAR DIARY
or
~~INTELLIGENCE SUMMARY~~
(Erase heading not required.)

139th Trench Mortar Battery

Place	Date	Hour	Summary of Events and Information	Remarks and references to Appendices
	1.7.18 to 4.7.18		Battery at rest at FOUQUIÈRES.	
	5.7.18 to 15.7.18		In the line EAST of BÈTHUNE. on the night of 15th by the 139th T.M. Bty, and moved back to FOUQUIÈRES	
	16.7.18 to 21.7.18		At FOUQUIÈRES, training in Physical Drill, and Gun Drill.	
	22.7.18 to 31.7.18		In the line EAST of BÈTHUNE.	

[illegible] Lieut
O.C. 139th T.M. Bty.

2449 Wt. W14957/M90 750,000 1/16 J.B.C. & A. Forms/C.2118/12.

Army Form C. 2118.

Instructions regarding War Diaries and Intelligence Summaries are contained in F. S. Regs., Part II. and the Staff Manual respectively. Title Pages will be prepared in manuscript.

WAR DIARY
or
~~INTELLIGENCE SUMMARY~~
(Erase heading not required.)

139th Trench Mortar Battery

Place	Date	Hour	Summary of Events and Information	Remarks and references to Appendices
	1.8.18 to 2.8.18		In the line EAST of BÈTHUNE. Relieved by the 137 T.M. Bty on the night of the 2nd, and moved back into Billets at FOUQUIÈRES	
	3.8.18 to 8.8.18		At Rest, at FOUQUIÈRES. On the night of the 8th the Battery moved into the line EAST of BÈTHUNE and relieved the 138 T.M. Bty.	
	9.8.18 to 20.8.18		In the line EAST of BETHUNE. Casualties whilst in the line this period, NIL. The Battery was relieved on the 20th by the 137th T.M.B.	
	21.8.18 to 26.8.18		At FOUQUIÈRES, training, Gun Drill, Physical Drill etc. moved into the line on the 26th and relieved the 138 T.M.B.	
	27.8.18 to 31.8.18		In the line EAST of BÈTHUNE.	

J.[illegible] Peacock
Captain
O.C. 139th T.M. Battery

2449 Wt. W14957/M90 750,000 1/16 J.B.C. & A. Forms/C.2118/12.

Instructions regarding War Diaries and Intelligence Summaries are contained in F. S. Regs., Part II. and the Staff Manual respectively. Title pages will be prepared in manuscript.

WAR DIARY

or

~~INTELLIGENCE SUMMARY.~~

(Erase heading not required.)

Army Form C. 2118.

130th Trench Mortar Battery

Place	Date	Hour	Summary of Events and Information	Remarks and references to Appendices
	1/9/18 to 4/9/18		In the GORRE SECTOR EAST of BETHUNE on the night of the 1st inst the Battery were relieved by the 178th T.M. By. & moved across & relieved the 137 T.M. By in the ESSARS SECTOR EAST of BETHUNE	Killed on the line N.W. ST QUENTIN the following [illegible] casualties [illegible]
	5/9/18 to 6/9/18		Battery was relieved by the 56 T.M.By. & moved back to rest billets BETHUNE	
			At BETHUNE	
	7/9/18		Battery moved to billets at AUCHEL	
	to 10/9/18		Training at AUCHEL (P.T. Gun Drill, Squad Drill, Ceremonial Drill, Advanced Gun Drill) were carried out each day.	[illegible]
	11/9/18		Battery entrained at CALONNE RICOUART for new area & detrained at CORBIE on the 12th inst,	[illegible]
	12/9/18		& marched to billets at FRANVILLERS.	
	13/9/18 to 17/9/18		Training at FRANVILLERS (Training with Mortars in conjunction with Battalions, Artillery formation & Extended Order Drill, Gun Drill, Route March)	[illegible] wounded 21/9/18
	18/9/18		Battery entrained for POEUILLY & arrived there on the morning of the 19th inst	
	19/9/18		At POEUILLY	[illegible] 20995 Pte E. Hutchinson Wounded 22/9/18
	20/9/18		Battery relieved the 2nd T.M.By in the line N.W. of ST. QUENTIN	
	to 25/9/18		In the line N.W. of ST. QUENTIN	
	26/9/18		Battery relieved by the 1st T.M.By & moved to CAMBRIERES WOODS.	
	27/9/18		In CAMBRIERE'S WOODS	
	28/9/18 to 30/9/18		Battery moved into the line N.W. of ST. QUENTIN	

[signature]
Captain
O.C. 130 Trench Mortar Battery

A7092). Wt. W12839/M1293 750,000. 1/17. D. D & L., Ltd. Forms/C2118/14.

Instructions regarding War Diaries and Intelligence Summaries are contained in F. S. Regs., Part II. and the Staff Manual respectively. Title pages will be prepared in manuscript.

WAR DIARY
or
INTELLIGENCE SUMMARY.
(Erase heading not required.)

Army Form C. 2118.

~~45~~ 46

HQ 139 Infy Bde

139 Trench Mortar Battery

App 1 Vol 44

Oct

Place	Date	Hour	Summary of Events and Information	Remarks and references to Appendices
	1/10/18 to 3/10/18		In the line N.W. of ST. QUENTIN.	During the period in the line the following became casualties. (All wounded)
	4/10/18		The Battery withdrew to MAGNY-LE-FOSSE	
	5/10/18		Battery relieved the 14th and 97th T.M.B. in the line N.W. of ST. QUENTIN.	203402 Pte Thorpe C.
	6/10/18		The Battery was withdrawn from the line to MAGNY-LE-FOSSE.	201772 L/Cpl Harvey F.
	9/10/18		Moved from MAGNY-LE-FOSSE to LERVERGIES.	267688 Pte Birch R.
	10/10/18		The Battery moved from LERVERGIES to BEAUVREGARD.	240321 Cpl Smith R.
	11/10/18		At BEAUVREGARD.	240388 Pte Rounds A.
	12/10/18		Training and reorganization was carried out during the morning.	240370 Pte Dawson J.
			In the afternoon the Battery moved to FRESNOY-LE-GRAND.	242568 Pte Roberts B
	13/10/18 to 15/10/18		Training at FRESNOY-LE-GRAND.	307613 Pte Morrissy J.
	16/10/18		The Battery moved into the line at REGNICOURT.	92053 Pte Garbutt G.
	18/10/18		The Battery withdrew from the line, and moved back to billets at FRESNOY-LE-GRAND.	
	19/10/18 to 30/10/18		Training at FRESNOY-LE-GRAND on the following lines. Cleaning. Reorganization. Tightening up of Discipline. Steadying Drill. Physical Drill. Gun Drill. Ceremonial Drill and Musketry.	
	30/10/18		Battery moved to BOHAIN	
	31/10/18		Training as on former lines.	

R. H. Wood Lieut.
Officer Commanding 139th Trench Mortar Battery

A7092) Wt. W12839/M1293 750,000. 1/17. D. D & L., Ltd. Forms/C2118/14.

Army Form C. 2118.

Instructions regarding War Diaries and Intelligence Summaries are contained in F. S. Regs., Part II. and the Staff Manual respectively. Title pages will be prepared in manuscript.

WAR DIARY

or

~~INTELLIGENCE SUMMARY.~~

(Erase heading not required.)

139th Trench Mortar Battery.

Place	Date	Hour	Summary of Events and Information	Remarks and references to Appendices
	1-11-18 to 2-11-18		Training at BOHAIN. } Inspection, Squad Drill, Rifle Exercises, Firing Practice with Mortars.	
	3-11-18 to 6-11-18		Battery moved to ESCAUFOURT and moved into the line on 6th inst. at CATTILLON	
	7-11-18		Battery was relieved in the line by 138th T.M.B & moved PETIT-FAYT	
	8-11-18		At PETIT-FAYT	
	9-11-18		Moved to BOULOGNE (S. EAST) of LANDRECIES.	
	10-11-18 to 13-11-18		At BOULOGNE	
	14-11-18		Moved to LANDRECIES	
	15-11-18 to 30-11-18		At LANDRECIES } Training, — P.T. Ceremonial Drill, Gun Drill, Rifle Exercises etc. Half Battery each day working in conjunction with Battalions in clearing up the Battle Fields.	

[signature]
Capt
Cdr. 139 Trench Mortar Battery

A7092). Wt. W12839/M1293 750,000. 1/17. D. D & L., Ltd. Forms/C2118/14.

Instructions regarding War Diaries and Intelligence Summaries are contained in F. S. Regs., Part II, and the Staff Manual respectively. Title pages will be prepared in manuscript.

Army Form C. 2118.

WAR DIARY
or
~~INTELLIGENCE SUMMARY.~~
(Erase heading not required.)

139 Trench Mortar Battery

Place	Date	Hour	Summary of Events and Information	Remarks and references to Appendices
	1-12-18 to 31-12-18		At LANDRECIES. } Training – P.T. Ceremonial Drill, Route March, Gun Drill, Rifle Exercises etc. Half the Battery each day working in conjunction with Battalions in clearing up the Battle Fields.	

Dickinson Capt
Oc. 139 Trench Mortar Battery

A7092). Wt. W12839/M1293 750,000. 1/17. D. D & L., Ltd. Forms/C2118/14.

Instructions regarding War Diaries and Intelligence Summaries are contained in F. S. Regs., Part II. and the Staff Manual respectively. Title pages will be prepared in manuscript.

WAR DIARY

or

~~INTELLIGENCE~~ SUMMARY.

(*Erase heading not required.*) 139 Trench Mortar Battery.

Army Form C. 2118.

Place	Date	Hour	Summary of Events and Information	Remarks and references to Appendices
	1-1-19 to 10-1-19		At LANDRECIES - Training - P.T. Ceremonial Drill, Route Marches + Rifle Exercises. Half the Battery working in conjunction with Battalions in clearing up the Battle Fields.	
	11-1-19.		The Battery moved to PRISCHES.	
	12-1-19 to 31-1-19		At PRISCHES. 50% of the Battery working daily on the Brigade Salvage Dump. Remaining 50% working 4 days per week in conjunction with the Battalions in clearing up the Battle Fields. On the remaining 2 days — P.T. Rifle Exercises. Route Marches and Baths.	

Dickinson Capt.

O. C. 139th Trench Mortar Battery.

A7092). Wt. W12839/M1293 750,000. 1/17. D. D & L., Ltd. Forms/C2118/14.

Instructions regarding War Diaries and Intelligence Summaries are contained in F. S. Regs., Part II. and the Staff Manual respectively. Title pages will be prepared in manuscript.

WAR DIARY

or

~~INTELLIGENCE SUMMARY.~~

(Erase heading not required.)

Army Form C. 2118.

Vol 48

Place	Date	Hour	Summary of Events and Information	Remarks and references to Appendices
~~LANDRECIES~~ PRISCHES	1.2.19 - 11.2.19		Continued Salvage.	(Ref Map 57A1/40 000)
	12.2.19		Brig. Genl. J Harington D.S.O. proceeded to BONN (Germany) on leave. Lt Col. H H. Stoney, D.S.O. assumed command of the Brigade	
	13.2.19 - 18.2.19		Continued Salvage.	
	19.2.19		The Brigade Groupe marched to CATILLON + BAZUEL	(57B1/40,000) App I
	20.2.19		do do BETHENCOURT.	
	21.2.19		Brig. Genl. J Harington returned from Germany + took over command of the Brigade.	
	22.2.19 - 28.2.19		Continued Salvage.	
			During the month, 718, all ranks, in the Brigade were demobilised.	

R.L.A. Comer Lieut
for Brigade Major
139 th Inf. Bde

A7092). Wt. W12839/M1293 750,000. 1/17. D. D & L., Ltd. Forms/C2118/14.

Army Form C. 2118.

Instructions regarding War Diaries and Intelligence Summaries are contained in F. S. Regs., Part II, and the Staff Manual respectively. Title pages will be prepared in manuscript.

WAR DIARY
or
~~INTELLIGENCE SUMMARY.~~
(Erase heading not required.)

139 Trench Mortar Battery.

Place	Date	Hour	Summary of Events and Information	Remarks and references to Appendices
	1/2/19 to 18/2/19		At PRISCHES. 50% of the Battery working daily on the Brigade Salvage Dump. Remaining 50% working 4 days per week in conjunction with the Battalions in clearing up the Battle Fields. The remaining 2 days P.T. Ceremonial Drill, Route Marches + Baths.	
	19/2/19		The Battery moved to CATTILON.	
	20/2/19		The Battery moved to BETHENCOURT	
	21/2/19 To 28/2/19		The Battery were engaged on the Brigade Salvage Dump.	

Dickinson Capt

D. D. & L., London, E.C. (A7853) Wt. W209/M1672 350,000 4/17 Sch. 52a Forms C/2118/14

139 INFANTRY BRIGADE WARNING ORDER No.232.

app I

****

The 139 Infantry Brigade Group will leave the PRISCHES Area on February 19th. The night 19/20th Feby. will be spent at CATILLON & BAZUEL.
On 20th February the Brigade Group will move to BETHENCOURT.

Captain.
Brigade Major, 139th Inf. Bde.

14.2.19.

Issued to : -

5th Sherwood Foresters.
6th Sherwood Foresters.
8th Sherwood Foresters.
139 T.M. Battery.
Brigade Signals.
Brigade Supply Officer.
454 Company A.S. C.
1/1st N.M.F.A.
Staff Captain.

M A R C H   T A B L E   TO ACCOMPANY 139 BRIGADE ORDER No. 233.

SERIAL NUMBER	A UNIT	B DATE	C FROM.	D TO.	E ROUTE.	F. REMARKS.
1.	5th Battn. S.F.	Feby. 19th	BEAUREPAIRE	CATILLON	ANY	To leave BEAUREPAIRE at 10.00 hours.
2.	6th " "	" "	CARTIGNIES.	"	"	" " CARTIGNIES at 10.00 "
3.	8th " "	" "	PRISCHES.	BAZUEL	"	To be clear of PRISCHES by 09 .45 hrs.
4.	1/1 N.M.F.A.	" "	"	CATILLON	"	To leave PRISCHES at 09.50 hours.
5.	139 T.M.Battery.	" "	"	"	"	To follow immediately in rear of 1/1st N. M.F.A.
6.	139 Bde H.Q.	" "	"	"	"	To leave PRISCHES at 10.00 hours.
7.	454 Coy.A.S.C.	" "	"	BETHENCOURT	"	To be clear of PRISCHES by 09.00 hrs
8.						
8.	5th Battn. S.F.	Feby 20th	CATILLON	BETHENCOURT	"	To be clear of CATILLON by 0 9.15 hr s.
9.	6th " "	" "	"	"	"	To leave CATILLON at 09.30 hrs.
10.	8th " "	" "	BAZUEL	"	"	To be clear of BAZUEL by 09.30 hrs.
11.	1/1 N.M.F.A.	" "	CATILLON	"	"	To leave CATILLON at 09.45 hrs.
12.	139 T.M.Battery.	" "	"	"	"	Follow immediately in rear of N.M.F.A.A
13.	139 Bde H.Q.	" "	"	"	"	To leave CATILLON at 10.00 hrs.

17th February 1919.

app I

139 BRIGADE ORDER No. 233.

Ref. Map. VALENCIENNES. 1/100,000. 17th Feby. 1919.

1. The 139 Brigade Group will march from PRISCHES Area to BETHENCOURT on February 19th and 20th in accordance with attached March Table.

2. Billeting parties for Units billeting in CATILLON will proceed independently and report to AREA COMMANDANT, Billet No. 28, CATILLON, who will allot. The 8th Sherwood Foresters will make their own arrangements to find the necessary ~~accommodat~~ accommodation in BAZUEL.

3. Baggae waggons fr 5th & 6th Sherwood Foresters will report on afternoon of 18th February. Waggons for 8th Sherwood Foresters and Brihade H.Q. will report by 07.30 hours on 19th inst.

4. Supplies for consumption on 20th inst., will be delivered to Units on arrival at CATILLON & BAZUEL. Supplies for consumption on 21st inst., will join Units on arrival at BETHENCOURT.

5. An Ambulance will call for men unable to march at H.Q. 5th, 6th & 8th Sherwood Foresters on morning of moves. Any other Units having men unable to march will send them to the nearest Battalion H.Q. A horse ambulance will move in rear of 6th Sherwood Foresters on the 19th inst., and in rear of Brigade H.Q. on the 20th inst.

6. Brigade H.Q. will close at 10.00 hours each day and will reopen at CATILLON & BETHENCOURT respectively on arrival.

7. Units of Brigade Group to ACKNOWLEDGE.

[signature]

Captain.
Brigade Major, 139th Infantry Brigade.

Issued to : -

5th, 6th, 8th Sherwood Foresters.
139 T.M.Battery.
Brigade Signals.
464 Company A S. C.
1/1st N.M.F. A.
46th Division.

5th Sherwood

Foresters

46

1/5 Notts & Derby Regt

Vol 12

139^h McGeoy

46

1/5 Notts & Derby Regt

Vol XI

46

1/8 Notts & Derby Regt

Feb

Vol XII

W.2.

8th Sherwood

Foresters

46

1/8 Notts & Derby Regt

Vol XIV

46

8 Notts & Derby

Vol XIII

13

46

139 Bde MGun Coy

Vol II

46

139 Bde M G Coy

Vol III

139 Bde M. Gun Coy

Feb

Vol I

www.ingramcontent.com/pod-product-compliance
Lightning Source LLC
Chambersburg PA
CBHW081242170426
43191CB00034B/2018
9781474525787